Let music swell the breeze,
And ring from all the trees
Sweet freedom's song.
Let mortal tongues awake;
Let all that breathe partake;
Let rocks their silence break,
The sound prolong.

Our fathers' God, to Thee,
Author of liberty,
To Thee we sing.
Long may our land be bright,
With freedom's holy light;
Protect us by Thy might,
Great God, our King!

JAN 1 5

My Country, 'Tis of Thee

How One Song Reveals the History of Civil Rights

CLAIRE RUDOLF MURPHY

Illustrated by

BRYAN COLLIER

Henry Holt and Company
New York

More than any other, one song traces America's history of patriotism and protest. Since 1831, Americans have sung "My Country, 'Tis of Thee" to honor the freedoms promised in the Declaration of Independence. Protesters for equal rights have claimed their place in this nation's history by writing and singing new verses.

The song first appeared in England in the 1740s as "God Save the King." Supporters of King George II sang it during a 1745 power struggle for the British throne.

God save our gracious King
Long live our noble King,
God save the King.
Send him victorious,
Happy and glorious,
Long to reign over us,
God save the King.

After Bonnie Prince Charlie, King George's rival, defeated English soldiers in Scotland, his followers sang a new verse to honor their hero's right to be king.

God bless the prince, I pray,
God bless the prince, I pray,
Charlie I mean;
That Scotland we may see
Freed from vile Presbyt'ry,
Both George and his Feckie,
Ever so, Amen.

Across the Atlantic, English colonists sang "God Save the King" at public gatherings.

9

British colonial soldiers sang the song to celebrate their victories in the French and Indian War. A charismatic preacher named George Whitefield popularized new verses set to the melody. He preached that all men are equal and should praise God together—rich and poor, white and black, including slaves.

Come, Thou Almighty King
Help us Thy name to sing,
Help us to praise.
Father! All-glorious
O'er all victorious
Come, and reign over us
Ancient of days.

Talk of liberty spread across the new land.

11

But colonists had no voice in Parliament. In 1765, King George III began taxing the colonists without their consent. Frustrated, they refused to buy goods from England and drank coffee or Dutch tea instead of English tea. Women wove their own fabric instead of using English linen, while men held secret meetings and dumped English tea in the harbor. Loyal colonists continued to sing the British verses, but angry citizens called for a revolution.

Fame, let thy Trumpet sound.
Rouse all the World around,
With loud alarms!
Fly hence to Britain's land,
Tell George in vain his Hand
Is raised 'gainst FREEDOM'S Band.
When call'd to arms.

On July 4, 1776, Americans declared themselves independent of England.

Early in the war, British soldiers and loyalists sang "God Save the King" after every victory. Revolutionary soldiers shouted their own new verses as they marched into battle. They dreamed of freedom and having a voice in their new country's government.

God save the Thirteen States!
Long rule the United States!
God save our States!
Make us victorious;
Happy and glorious;
No tyrants over us;
God save our States!

Seven years later, the colonists finally
won their independence.

A new country was formed—the United States of America. Its leaders wrote a Constitution that promised justice and liberty for all. White male landowners elected the first president. Song-writers wrote dozens of new verses to celebrate the new country and the new president. In 1789, Americans serenaded President George Washington in New York City on his Inauguration Day.

Hail, thou auspicious day!
Far let America
Thy praise resound:
Joy to our native land!
Let ev'ry heart expand,
For Washington's at hand,
With glory crown'd!

But it was not an auspicious day for everyone.

For years, women like Abigail Adams had encouraged leaders to "Remember the Ladies" when they wrote our country's new laws. But the men did not listen. In most states, women were not free to vote, to own property, or to make important decisions about their children's lives. In 1795, an anonymous woman published this protest verse in a Philadelphia newspaper.

God save each Female's right,
Show to her ravished sight
Woman is Free;
Let Freedom's voice prevail,
And draw aside the veil,
Supreme Effulgence hail,
Sweet Liberty.

**Many still did not believe that women
deserved the same freedoms as men.**

Americans celebrated their new country every year on the Fourth of July. But they had no national anthem to sing. In 1831, a seminary student named Samuel Francis Smith wrote patriotic verses to a melody he found in an old German hymnal. He had no idea his new song shared the same tune as "God Save the King." At the Independence Day service, the children's choir at Park Street Church in Boston debuted the song Smith called "America."

My native country, thee,
Land of the noble free,
Thy name I love.
I love thy rocks and rills,
Thy woods and templed hills;
My heart with rapture thrills
Like that above.

But black children could only listen
from the back of the church.

America was not a *"land of the noble free"* for the four million slaves in the South. Calling for an end to slavery, abolitionists wrote hundreds of protest verses to well-known tunes. They were sung at rallies and meetings across the land.

My country, 'tis for thee,
Dark land of slavery,
For thee I weep.
Land where the slave has sighed,
And where he toil'd and died,
To serve a tyrant's pride,
For thee I weep.

But slavery did not end.

In 1861, the Civil War broke out between the North and the South over slavery and states' rights. Northern soldiers sang "America" as they marched into battle.

Let music swell the breeze,
And ring from all the trees
Sweet freedom's song.
Let mortal tongues awake;
Let all that breathe partake;
Let rocks their silence break,
The sound prolong.

Southern soldiers sang different verses, such as "God Save the South." Civilians on both sides performed old and new verses at public parades and around the piano at home.

Then, 'mid the cannon's roar
Let us Sing evermore:
God Save the South!
Ours is the soul to dare;
See, our good swords are bare—
We will be free, we swear!
God save the South!

Thousands of Yankee and Rebel soldiers died as the war dragged on.

When President Abraham Lincoln's 1863 Emancipation Proclamation ended slavery in the Confederate states, he and Mrs. Lincoln sang "America" with soldiers and freed slaves at Union battle camps. And when the war finally ended in 1865, free black people sang new verses at joyous celebrations.

Come sing a cheerful lay,
And celebrate this day
Throughout the land.
Oh! Let us joyful be,
For freedom's sons are we,
In this land now the free
At thy command.

In 1870, *"freedom's sons"* of color
gained a voice through voting, too.

In the decades following the Civil War, protesters supporting many causes wrote new lyrics to the country's favorite melody. Labor activists believed that equal rights meant better working conditions, higher pay, an eight-hour workday, and an end to child labor.

My country, 'tis of thee,
Once land of liberty,
Of thee I sing.
Land of the Millionaire;
Farmers with pockets bare;
Caused by the cursed snare—
The Money Ring.

Their protests helped pass laws that improved working conditions.

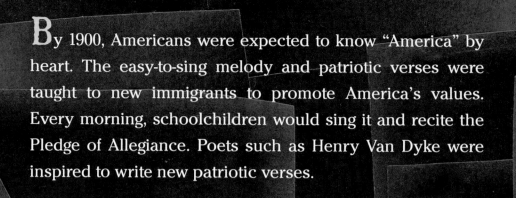

By 1900, Americans were expected to know "America" by heart. The easy-to-sing melody and patriotic verses were taught to new immigrants to promote America's values. Every morning, schoolchildren would sing it and recite the Pledge of Allegiance. Poets such as Henry Van Dyke were inspired to write new patriotic verses.

I love thine inland seas,
Thy groves of giant trees,
Thy rolling plains;
Thy rivers' mighty sweep,
Thy mystic canyons deep,
Thy mountains wild and steep,
All thy domains.

But "America" was not chosen
as the national anthem. The tune to
"God Save the King" would not do.

In 1868, men of color were allowed to vote. But not freedom's daughters—black or white. Women sang new verses, demanding their right to the ballot box. And they kept on singing and marching until all women won the right to vote in 1920.

Our country, now from thee
Claim we our liberty,
In freedom's name.
Guarding home's altar fires,
Daughters of patriot sires,
Their zeal our own inspires,
Justice to claim.

BALLOT

BOX

But the privilege to vote didn't extend to
Native Americans, male or female.

Even though American Indians had lived on this land for thousands of years, they still were not considered citizens of the United States. In 1919, Sioux writer Zitkala-Ša protested by publishing her poem "A Red Man's America."

My country! 'Tis to thee,
Sweet land of Liberty,
My pleas I bring.
Land where OUR fathers died,
Whose offspring are denied
The Franchise given wide,
Hark, while I sing.

Equality did not exist
for everyone in America.

People of color were not treated as full citizens. They couldn't attend the same schools, eat at the same restaurants, or shop at the same stores as white Americans. In 1939, opera star Marian Anderson wasn't allowed to sing inside Constitution Hall in Washington, D.C., so she sang on the steps of the Lincoln Memorial in front of 75,000 people. In protest and in patriotism, she performed America's favorite song but changed two words. She sang *for all* her country's people, in hopes that her nation would become a place of liberty for all.

My country, 'tis of thee,
Sweet land of liberty,
For thee we sing.
Land where my fathers died!
Land of the pilgrims' pride!
From every mountainside,
Let freedom ring!

Millions of Americans, including ten-year-old Martin Luther King Jr., listened on the radio.

In 1944, fifteen-year-old Martin Luther King Jr. won a contest with his speech "The Negro and the Constitution." It featured the story of Anderson's inspiring concert. "Black America still wears chains. . . . Miss Anderson may not as yet spend the night in any good hotel in America."

Nineteen years later, during the March on Washington, King himself stood in front of the Lincoln Memorial. "I have a dream," his voice rang out.

This will be the day
when all of God's children
will be able to sing with new meaning:
"My country, 'tis of thee,
sweet land of liberty, of thee I sing. . . .

From every mountainside
let freedom ring."

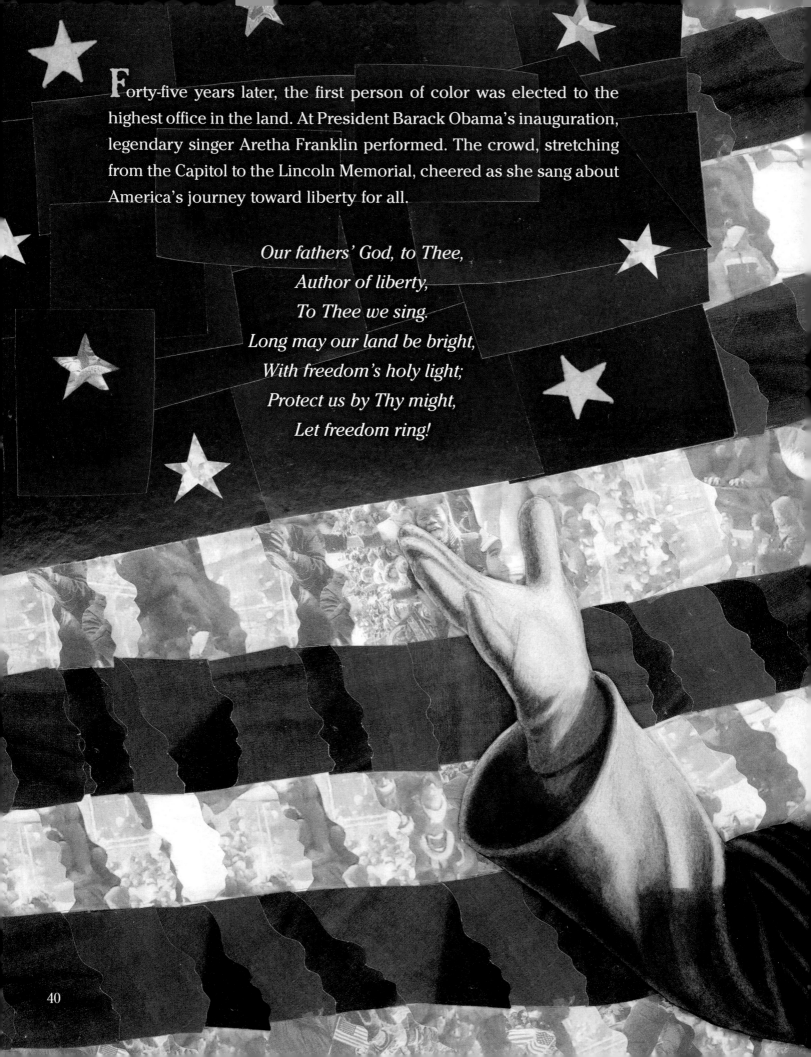

Forty-five years later, the first person of color was elected to the highest office in the land. At President Barack Obama's inauguration, legendary singer Aretha Franklin performed. The crowd, stretching from the Capitol to the Lincoln Memorial, cheered as she sang about America's journey toward liberty for all.

Our fathers' God, to Thee,
Author of liberty,
To Thee we sing.
Long may our land be bright,
With freedom's holy light;
Protect us by Thy might,
Let freedom ring!

Now it's your turn. Write a new verse for a cause you believe in. *Help freedom ring.*

41

Source Notes

pp. 6-7: While researching the women's suffrage movement, I uncovered a set of suffrage-themed verses to "My Country, 'Tis of Thee." I wondered whether other protest movements had also written verses to this tune. My journey led me to the book *Sweet Freedom's Song*, by Robert Branham and Stephen Hartnett.

I have since discovered that "America" is likely the best-known tune in the world. It has been, at one time or another, the melody for twenty nations' anthems.

pp. 8-9: "God Save the King" was first published in the 1744 music collection *Thesaurus Musicus*. Some historians believe the melody came from the French hymn "Domine Salvum Fac Regem" and credit the lyrics to Henry Carey, but many believe the origin is unknown.

Prince Charles Edward Stuart, popularly known as Bonnie Prince Charlie, was the grandson of James II, who was overthrown as king of England in 1688 and exiled to France. Bonnie Prince Charlie's verses are featured in *The Union Jack: The Story of the British Flag*. The name "Feckie" refers to King George II's son Frederick, the Prince of Wales.

pp. 10-11: During the French and Indian War (1754-1763), Great Britain fought with France over territory in the New World. The 1757 hymn with new verses, popular in both England and the colonies, became known as "Whitefield's Tune." In 1769, the melody was altered, and the hymn has been known ever since as "Come, Thou Almighty King."

pp. 12-13: King George III needed funds to pay for the French and Indian War, so the British Parliament passed the 1765 Stamp Act, which assessed a tax on all legal documents and printed materials such as newspapers. Angry colonists wrote hundreds of protest lyrics set to familiar tunes. Most were published

anonymously so the writer would not be thrown in jail. The *Boston Independent Chronicle* published this verse, entitled "A New Song."

pp. 14-15: The authorship of "God Save the Thirteen States," published in January 1780 in the newspaper the *Pennsylvania Packet*, is credited to "a Dutch Lady at the Hague." The complete verses can be found at *Lyrics to Songs of Freedom* (www.mcgath .com/freelyr.html).

pp. 16-17: "Ode to Be Sung on the Arrival of the President of the United States," by Samuel Low, was handed out on broadsides to the crowd and published in the *Gazette of the United States* on April 25, 1789, and in other newspapers throughout the spring and summer. The complete verses can be found in *Sweet Freedom's Song*.

pp. 18-19: On March 31, 1776, Abigail Adams wrote a letter to her husband, John, who was attending the Continental Congress in Philadelphia. "In the new code of laws . . . I desire you would Remember the Ladies, and be more generous and favourable to them than your ancestors." The complete text can be found at the PBS *American Experience* website (http://www.pbs.org/wgbh/amex/adams/filmmore /ps_ladies.html).

The poem "Rights of Women: A Lady's Version of God Save the King" appeared in the women's magazine the *Philadelphia Minerva* on October 17, 1795. All ten verses can be found in *Sweet Freedom's Song*.

pp. 20-21: The new song was first published in an 1832 hymn collection. Dr. Smith (1808-1895) wrote some 150 hymns. But "America," written when he was only twenty-three years old, is his most famous. The song soon became better known as "My Country, 'Tis of Thee," possibly because so many other songs and poems contain "America" in the title.

In 1831 Boston, transportation, public buildings, and churches were still divided along the color line. The July 9 edition of the *Liberator* newspaper reported this about the song's premiere: "The colored boys were permitted to occupy pews one fourth of the way up the side aisle," while "the colored girls took their seats by the door, as usual."

pp. 22–23: The abolition verse can be found in *Protest Songs in America*.

Improvements to the steam-powered rotary printing press in the 1840s helped the abolitionist movement expand by making antislavery songbooks more available, especially to churchgoers and youth groups.

pp. 24–25: New verses were published in pocket songbooks, with lyrics celebrating the bravery of individual regiments, reporting on battles, and lauding or criticizing military and political leaders. Chaplain J. F. Mines of the Second Maine Regiment wrote the Union soldiers' verse in 1864. "God Save the South" appeared in an 1862 edition of the *Richmond Dispatch*.

pp. 26–27: Information about Abraham Lincoln and the song can be found in *They Knew Lincoln*. The verse "Song of Freedom" was published in the April 1863 edition of *Douglass' Monthly*.

pp. 28–29: "A New National Anthem" by Thomas Nicol is one of many versions of "America" that attacks the greed and corruption of factory, farm, and mine owners who cared only about making money rather than the rights and safety of their workers. At the time, laborers were forced to work six days a week, up to sixteen hours a day. This version was published in the 1891 *Alliance and Labor Songster*.

pp. 30–31: Henry Van Dyke's verses were published in *The White Bees: And Other Poems* in 1909. "My Country, 'Tis of Thee" was the nation's bestselling record in 1899. Recordings of the song beginning in the 1890s popularized it even more. It was sung at patriotic events and flag ceremonies until 1931, when Congress chose "The Star-Spangled Banner" as the national anthem.

pp. 32-33: The verse "The New America" was written by suffrage leader Elizabeth Boynton Harbert and is featured in the *Booklet of Song: A Collection of Suffrage and Temperance Melodies*.

pp. 34–35: Zitkala-Ša (Red Bird), also known as Gertrude Simmons Bonnin (1876–1938), was a writer, composer, and activist for American Indian rights. Her poem was published in the *American Indian Magazine*, and all verses were reprinted in her book *American Indian Stories, Legends, and Other Writings*. For more about her life, see Doreen Rappaport's biography for young readers *The Flight of Red Bird*.

pp. 36–37: American opera singer Marian Anderson (1897–1993) performed in concert halls all over Europe. For more information on her musical career, see the Penn Library online exhibit, *Marian Anderson: A Life in Song* (library.upenn.edu/exhibits/rbm/anderson/index.html#toc). You will find the 1939 performance and news report, as well as other performances by Marian Anderson, on YouTube.com.

pp. 38–39: For information on the 1944 speech Martin Luther King Jr. gave in high school, see "The Negro and the Constitution" on the Martin Luther King Jr. Research and Education Institute website. There are many links to both audio and text versions of his "I Have a Dream" speech online; you will find them if you do a Web search.

pp. 40–41: At President Barack Obama's inauguration on January 20, 2009, Aretha Franklin wore a hat that some speculate was modeled after the headdresses of slave women in the eighteenth and nineteenth centuries. It definitely celebrated the churchgoing finery that African-American women have worn for generations. You can watch her performance on YouTube.com.

Bibliography

Branham, Robert James, and Stephen J. Hartnett. *Sweet Freedom's Song: "My Country 'Tis of Thee" and Democracy in America.* New York: Oxford University Press, 2002.

Collins, Ace. *Songs Sung Red, White, and Blue: The Stories Behind America's Best-Loved Patriotic Songs.* New York: HarperCollins, 2003.

Groom, Nick. *The Union Jack: The Story of the British Flag.* London: Atlantic Books, 2006.

Rosen, David M. *Protest Songs in America.* Westlake Village, CA: Aware Press, 1972.

Washington, John E. *They Knew Lincoln.* New York: E. P. Dutton and Co., Inc., 1942.

Wheeler, L. May. *Booklet of Song: A Collection of Suffrage and Temperance Melodies.* Minneapolis, MN: Co-operative Printing Company, 1884.

Zitkala-Ša, *American Indian Stories, Legends, and Other Writings*, 2nd Edition. New York: Penguin, 2003 (originally published 1921).

Further Resources

If You Want to Learn More

For an article on the song, see the Library of Congress's Performing Arts Encyclopedia web page article, "My Country 'Tis of Thee" (lcweb2 .loc.gov/diglib/ihas/loc.natlib.ihas.200000012 /default.html).

For more Revolutionary War songs, visit the Carpenters' Hall website page "Songs of the Revolution" (ushistory.org/carpentershall/edu/songs.htm).

For more abolitionist songs, visit the "Abolition" page of the Library of Congress's online exhibit, The African-American Mosaic (loc.gov/exhibits /african/afam005.html).

For more information on Zitkala-Ša, look for *The Flight of Red Bird: The Life of Zitkala-Ša*, by Doreen Rappaport (Puffin Books, 1999).

For more labor songs, look for *The Alliance and Labor Songster: A Collection of Labor and Comic Songs, for the Use of Alliances, Grange Debating Clubs and Political Gatherings*, by Leopold Vincent (originally published by Vincent Bros., 1891; reprinted by Arno Press, 1975).

To read Henry Van Dyke's version of the song, as well as other poems by him, look for *The White Bees: And Other Poems*, by Henry Van Dyke (Charles Scribner's Sons, 1909).

For more women's suffrage songs, visit the "Suffrage Singalong!" page at CreativeFolk.com (creativefolk.com/suffrage.html).

For more information on Marian Anderson, look for *The Voice That Challenged a Nation: Marian Anderson and the Struggle for Equal Rights*, by Russell Freedman (Clarion Books, 2004).

For more information on Aretha Franklin, look for *Aretha Franklin: Lady Soul*, by Leslie Gourse (Franklin Watts, 1995).

Musical Links

For musical performances of all the protest verses, visit ClaireRudolfMurphy.com.

You'll find hundreds of renditions of "My Country, 'Tis of Thee" on YouTube.com, including one by the Air Force rock band Top Cover that features some new verses (youtube.com /watch?v=zDsVAL7DJ8g); a classical performance featuring the Mormon Tabernacle Choir (youtube.com/watch?v=zKZg_ZB4SkU); and a guitar lesson that features some of the song's history (youtube.com/watch?v=JcORzuZIvdw).

In memory of Debbie Tassey Moses (1952–2012),
who sang joyfully every day of her life
—C. R. M.

ACKNOWLEDGMENTS

For my agent, Kendra Marcus, and editor, Sally Doherty, who both believed in this project from the beginning; Samantha Mandel for her editorial assistance; Marc Aronson for his perceptive editorial comments; the Hamline MFAC community of students and faculty, who sang along in great spirit; and the Spokane writers, who supported this book's journey to publication: Mary Douthitt, Meghan Nuttall Sayres, Mary Cronk Farrell, and Kelly Milner Halls. And always to my husband, Murph; children, Conor and Meg; new son-in-law, Paul; the extended Murphy and Rudolf families; and my beloved mom, Frances Claire, who passed away before this book came into the world.

Henry Holt and Company, LLC
Publishers since 1866
175 Fifth Avenue
New York, New York 10010
mackids.com

Henry Holt® is a registered trademark of Henry Holt and Company, LLC.
Text copyright © 2014 by Claire Rudolf Murphy
Illustrations copyright © 2014 by Bryan Collier
All rights reserved.
Musical arrangement copyright © 2008 by Creative Commons Public Domain Dedication (USA);
Source: Dykema, Peter, et al. *I Hear America Singing: 55 Songs and Choruses
for Community Singing.* L.L. Birchard & Company, 1917.

Library of Congress Cataloging-in-Publication Data
Murphy, Claire Rudolf.
My country, 'tis of thee : how one song reveals the history of civil rights /
Claire Rudolf Murphy ; illustrated by Bryan Collier. — First edition.
pages   cm
Includes bibliographical references.
ISBN 978-0-8050-8226-5 (hardcover)
1. Smith, Samuel Francis, 1808–1895. America—Juvenile literature. 2. Political ballads and songs—United States—History
and criticism—Juvenile literature. 3. God save the King—Juvenile literature. I. Collier, Bryan, illustrator. II. Title.
ML3561.A5M87 2014   782.42'15990973—dc23   2013034387

Henry Holt books may be purchased for business or promotional use.
For information on bulk purchases, please contact the Macmillan Corporate and Premium Sales
Department at (800) 221-7945 x5442 or by e-mail at specialmarkets@macmillan.com.

First Edition—2014 / Designed by Patrick Collins
The artist used watercolor and collage to create the illustrations for this book.
Printed in China by South China Printing Co., Ltd., Dongguan City, Guangdong Province

1 3 5 7 9 10 8 6 4 2

America

(better known by its first line, "My Country, 'Tis of Thee")

Written by Samuel Francis Smith, 1831